DESMOND EGAN   PENINSUL

DESMOND EGAN

"Peninsula"

poems of the Dingle Peninsula
with photographs by LIAM LYONS

1992

THE KAVANAGH PRESS LTD. IRELAND

Published by
THE KAVANAGH PRESS Ltd.
Newbridge Co. Kildare Ireland

First edition 1992
ISBN 1-870491-55-6

The publishers gratefully acknowledge the sponsorship of
KODAK (Ireland) Ltd.

ACKNOWLEDGMENTS
The publishers would like to thank
Ms. Bernadette Smyth
Mr. Tom Murphy
Ms. Vivienne Abbott
Mr. Liam Lyons
for generous help given in the production of this book.

Printed by Goodson Print Ltd. — Tel: 304447

EPILOGUE

out the window of my study
Papel rasgado de um intento
a leaden March morning gives
and blue tatters show
there's a crow gawking from a bare tree
a volley from an unseeable blackbird

and for no reason I remember Kerry
the long road of stillness
An Fheóthanach shivering with daylight
the perspective to the Sisters
mist heights a view of abandoned ocean
somebody's voice coming a long way
life draining from a hill

landscape of tragic faces
where time fades to eternity

that great grey movement
over us all

Papel ... The torn paper of a draft : from a poem by Fernando Pessoa.
An Fheóthanach: place name, Feohanagh.

By DESMOND EGAN

POETRY

Midland (1972)
Leaves (1974)
Siege! (1977)
Woodcutter (1978)
Athlone? (1980)
Seeing Double (1983)
Snapdragon (1983, 1991)
Poems for Peace (1986)
A Song For My Father (1989)
Peninsula (1992)

Collected Poems (1983, 1984)
Selected Poems (Edited by Hugh Kenner) (1992)

TRANSLATION

Euripides, *Medea* (1991)

PROSE

The Death of Metaphor Selected Prose (1990, 1991)

IN TRANSLATION

Terre et Paix (French/English) (1988)
Echobogen (Dutch/English) (1990)
Quel Sole Storno Che Gelido Passa (Italian/English) (1992)

CRITICAL STUDY

Desmond Egan: The Poet and His Work
(Edited by Hugh Kenner, U.S.A. 1990)
Desmond Egan: A Critical Introduction by Brian Arkins (U.S.A. 1992)

Contents

For
Johnny Granville

and for
John Patrick Sullivan

FARMER NEAR SYBIL POINT

folded-in on himself like the peninsula
unlonely although
full of an unreachable gloom
he heads through a gate under

mountains of no illusion

WESTWARDS

an edge everywhere
something at stake in
this distilled brightness
those mountains surging
the remote valley
these aggressions of the sea

someone walking along a cliff

FEOHANAGH

bog cotton which lent its name
trembles here out of time

gables plots a school the pub
this turn of the road the signpost
directing to elsewhere

Ballyga tower still at lookout
making natives of us all

holy Mount Brandon and
Masatiompan in mist

a stretch of high reeds
soughing with life

and under falls of imagination
that startling blue continent
explored by a speck

Feohanagh: from the Irish word for bog cotton

IN JOHNNY GRANVILLE'S HOUSE

awakened by seaside brightness
raging through blinds the chill an

echo in light

when I glance out the kitchen door
there's a promontory of raw morning
with canyons of space blue distance rock
the white of an egg

I would drive more than 200 miles
for such a breakfast

DINGLE

somehow it never became a *resort*
but kept with its lanes that
puzzling Kerry handshake

the owner of a small supermarket
pointing directions with his butcher's cleaver

carnival of rain

a fishmonger's closed door

waves jumping beyond pubs and masts
at a hulk abandoned like the season

the silo of ice and
tenuous female streets
where ghosts of tourists
stalk without cameras

CORCA DHUIBHNE

in its mountainous spaces   rain sweeps cross-valley
each house stands isolate   cloud cold

in its atlantic light   such undeciphered ogham
                                   forever on whatever people are

COOSAKNOCKAUN

utter stillness
of one small boat glimpsed out
off the cliffs
on top of the incomprehensible sea

I am an outsider

KILFOUNTAN

has a feel to it a
souterrain quickening
some wholeness all its own

one of those places where
belief might earth itself

and ogham and cross converge
in one graceful pillar

DUN AN OIR

A sequence

(for Michael Murphy and Eileen Dunne)

A Dhia atá fial, a thruath na mbeannachta,
Féach na Gaeil go léir gan bharanta....*

        Fear Dorcha O Mealláin *An Díbirt go Connachta*

1

five ships at anchor
pinnaces over
the ropes of water

a galleon foaming in
its Papal ensign slapping
with hope to the silent Irish
watching from cliffs

from centuries

Dún an Oir in Smerwick Harbour was the site of a massacre of six hundred men, women and children in 1580 after a Papal expedition of Spaniards (mainly) Italians and Irish surrendered to Lord Deputy Grey.
*God who are generous, compassionate with blessings
See how the Irish are all dispossessed ...
(from *The Banishment to Connaught*, 17th Century poem by O'Mealláin).

11

under no flag
their weapons surrendered the surrounded
very ragged and a great part boys
reason in the wrong languages
por favor por favor
per favore
discovering their despair

as Ireland will for many a lifetime
from English soldiery fixing bayonet
testing the knot

no man no woman no crying child
will be allowed wriggle out
the inlet will do for pithead

weasel-eyed Raleigh leads a young girl
back to the fold
Oh cruel Time, which takes in trust
Our youth, our joys, and all we have
the looting and drinking is almost done
and drunken anger closing-in

and already the ropes are out
and already the swords are swishing
and steel thrusts into the screams
and hammers thud from the forge
where they brought Father Moore

➢

---

very ragged ... letter from Sir Richard Bingham to Walsingham, 1580
Oh cruel ... from *Nature That Washed Her Hands In Milk* by Sir Walter Raleigh (1552-1618)

no that is not the screeching of gulls
no that is not the pleading of the wind

Grey takes his daily constitutional
bringing Zouche and Bingham for company

occasionally they stop as he make a point

and back at his quarters
he gazes at thumb and forefinger
searching for a word

111

you can feel it still
the desolation

of Spaniards Italians as they realised
death had sailed from home
which they will never see again

of native Irish exiled by suffering
muttering stoic *Ar nAthairs*

of women and children encircled by
Grey's faith and *Raleigh's mercy*

you can hear the blades mowing
the sound a head makes or a throat
the thumping muffled by bone

listen
sand files back from round the stone

and there are other presences that shall not escape

Elizabeth's ready generals her soldiers
so prone to *revelling and spoiling* before
getting down to serious business
Elizabeth's grim Deputy so strong of stomach
Elizabeth's pet poet

➢

Ar nAthairs : *Our Fathers*
revelling ... letter from Bingham to Lane, 1580

bald Elizabeth herself
a gloss on *this late enterprise performed by you*
so greatly to Our liking

after the few women had been raped
one more time and decapitated like chickens
after the last head tossed to the cove
and body unroped heeled out
after the final child sworded-through
the sledgehammers dropped did
Raleigh and Macworth escort Grey
across the spongy land
to inspect the remains of the agreement and
did they advert to the wint'ry beauty as Phoebus
hid his wat'ry locks beyond the
shoals of corpses?

in the crying of these fields

this late enterprise ... letter from Queen Elizabeth to Lord Grey, 1580

IV

féach an rópa ar an gcroch !
a Thiarna Dia
táid chun sinne Gaeil a chrochadh
a Dhia a Dhia a Mhuire na ngrást
agus na mná? agus na páistí

Daidi! a Dhaidi
lig leis más é do thoil é
níor dhein se tada
achainím impím ort
ná cuir an rud sin air
ná ná ná ná ná
sin é mo Dhaidi
mo Dhaidi

dove é San Giuseppe?
che cosa face
ho studiato a Firenze
mi padre! mi madre!
perché perché perché?

an Gearaltach mallaithe
cá bhfuil an cladhaire anois?
agus and t-Iodáileach olc sin
bhain se an claidheamh d' ár lámhaibh
agus sháith sé Trócaire Raleigh ina áit
tá mo phort seinnte fiú gan troid

A Dhia atá fial, a thruath na mbeannactha,
Féach na Gaeil go léir gan bharanta

Papish dirt! here
try this English rope for size

heave ho my hearties

in ainm an Athar agus an Mhic
agus and Spioraid Naoimh
creidim i nDia
an tAthair Uilechumhachtach
Cruthaitheóir neimhe agus talmhan

bhí cónaí ar mo shinsear annseo
le fada an bhliain
ach anois tá mo shráidbhaile dóite
mo mhóinfhéar dubh agaibh
mo chlann scaipithe
is cuma liom bás nó beatha
níl sa bheatha a dfhág sibh againn
ach sórt báis
fágaidh mé an saol dorcha seo
gan bhrón

go tapaidh a Mháire bhig
síos leat ar an gcosán san
le taobh na h-aille
sar a dtagann siad thar n-ais
ag lorg níos mó díghe
slán agus beannacht a mhúirnín
go tapaidh ! cloisim arís iad
ag iompar na gcorpán

madre de Dios! mira los Irlandeses
señor señor por favor
tengo monedas para ti

éist éist
tá an dorchadas mór ag caoineadh

m'fhear m'fhear
tabhair dom m'fhear breá
a shaighdiúirí caoine
ná ná déanaigí é sin
a Mhuire a Mháthair Dé

trócaire trócaire trócaire
níl aon arm agam
cad mar gheall ar an gcomhrac?

is athair mé mar thú féin
tógaigí bhur lámha díom
cladhairí
neamh-fhir
madraí
tabhair mo phíce dom a mheatacháin
agus déanfaidh mé troid leat
a phéist
go h-Ifreann libh go léir
a Iosa Críost
cabhraigh liom anois

Irish shit! fight back would you?
now how do you feel eh?

éist leis an speachaíl
na daoine bochta
táim-se ag dul as mo mheabhair
tabharfaidh mé léim amach ó'n aill
b'fhearr liom é sin
ná an céasadh uafásach seo

déan trócaire
déan trócaire
tóg do láimh uaim-se
a Dhia a Dhia

fan in aice liom a Thomáis a mhic
ní chuirfidh siad isteach ort
creid ionnam
ní ligfidh mé dóibh é
fan liom a leinbh
fan liom-sa

eviva il Papa!

go saoraidh Dia Eire bhocht

For translations see Appendix, p. 69

V

dispatch penned for the Deputy in
most careful and beautiful italic
Spenser gets down to *the writin'*

in his bivouac he explores
vellum and chair the canvas wall

across a dying november evening
he can discern hardly any screaming now

he dips quill begins to scratch
a phrase into *The Teares of the Muses*

And ye Faire Ladie th'honor of your daies
And glorie of the world, your high thoughts scorne,
Vouchsafe this moniment of his last praise
With some few silver dropping teares t'adorne:
And as ye be of heauenlie off-spring borne,
So unto heauen let your high mind aspire
And loathe this drosse of sinful worlds desire.

---

most careful ... description by Renwick, editor of *A View of the State of Ireland* by Spenser (1596).
right column: Spenser, from *The Ruines of Time*. (These lines are addressed Queen Elizabeth I).

V1

blood on the grass
horror under the fern

evening swings like a body
the mist is cold as steel
death stinks from the bay

no bird will sing
at Ard na Caithne
nor no wave wash
away what remains

éist éist
the cliff screams at Ard na Ceartan

KILMALKEDAR

retreat through romanesque
the tympanum moulded by a different mind

and facing the motionless ever-moving
ridge of Reenconnell
allow the medieval light
into your own recesses

if your soul can
squeeze through the east window
you will get to heaven

East window: called *Cró na Snathaide* /The Eye of the Needle.

GALLARUS

an upturned boat no Parthenon but
this temple in the local gritstone
also adheres with faith for mortar

stoop under its heavy lintel step
into an age of illumination

light from the eighth century still
splays from the east into our gloom

take time enough to be there
this is a serious place

an idea moulded along
Platonic lines coaxed out of masonry
when it and the fingers the hope cohered

watertight

THE THREE SISTERS

these fins out of outer history
one after another after another

lend the remoteness between
here and the real fall

that challenge of
vaguely sensed
possibilities

TOURISTS

the retired farmer who
tried to get us the key after midnight

looks over from his morning bungalow
laughs gives a wave and goes in

with that delighful
Kerry delay

rucksacks cars cameras sunglasses
revv into the landscape

never to be loved
among these eternities

KERRY

as little in need of music
(a fiddle flailing through noise)
as Sicily

not for lovers either
its grin middleaged

but sustained by its own truth
some continuum

a recession of peaks

DOONEEN PIER

wend your way down
past the tarred currachs on blocks
the green netting
the rampart of stones and thrift
the clamps of lobsterpots
the mackerel heads their accepting eyes

walk the high walled slipway
between sea and sea

to inhale it all

absorb the cold sound and
get the whiff of an element foreign to most

begin to admit those
frightening levels the breezes

of a necessity I only came to recognise
returning in a *naomhóg* from the Blaskets
seeing visitors growing along the pier

---

naomhóg: a hand-made currach for three, of a shape peculiar to the South-West

NAOMHOG

through its tarred skin
you can discern the lattice slats
as the two brothers pull out
up down up

afloat in a consciousness

where no one can reach them

BALLYFERRITER

Piaras Ferriter's town!
and the vowels still have the sea
the consonants rock in them
the sentences a ghost of the rhythm
of a civilisation

that old wonderful resistance

Irish in the supermarket
but there's a feel of absence

and Fáilte Abhaile on a streamer
over the fire in O Muircheartaigh's bar

the songs are songs of exile

has there been a pining
since Piaras died and Sybil
and the 600 at Dún an Oir

with no sea no river
to lighten the loss?

sad Ballyferriter where it always rains

Piaras Ferriter, an important Irish poet, was also the last of the 17th. century chieftains to hold out against the English; he
was hanged in Killarney in 1653. Sybil Lynch eloped with one of the Ferriter family and drowned accidentally while hiding
in a cave beneath the castle.
Fáilte Abhaile : welcome home.

RIASC

veet veet goes a plover
dissolving into
bare mountain
bare sea
bare perspectives of fields

bare faces

LATEEVEMORE

you can still identify the ridges
of *lazybeds* untouched since famine
starved both digger and the will

of a people who hope for little
forget nothing and
make no easy act of faith

the skipper of a fishing boat
ploughing contemptuously out

---

lazybeds : potato beds piled-up rather than dug

BALLYNAGALL STRAND

light is ebbing and
its failing pathway
gilt silver
leads wet sand out towards the
mystery of the bay

and everything becomes

one
again

THE GREAT BLASKET

its authority
slowly drew us in

but the slipway was in moss
those proud cottages sagging
inwards like Irish and

the winds of Europe
blew through blank windows

O Criomhthain
Peig
Muirís O Súilleabháin

I waited on a cliff-height for
for some sign from mainland Ireland

began to understand why mediocrity
never became the norm out here
where existence is an exile
➤

mist islands
a feel of the tremendous
sea through the currach's skin

the imaginary crash of surf
whitening in the distance

cold of a summer morning

and nothing but elements
to add to a quarter century

past *An Tráth Bhán* icy waters
still coursed through the Sound and
over the ships of history

dear dear place
empty in the last mild collapse
of a once-great Gaelic vision
which persisted into our time

SLEA HEAD

gannets shoot off the cliff face wait
in the wind and emptiness outside
big as geese eyeing downwards for
a twist of silver under the surface

and lunge with folding black plunging
unstoppable through the skin
into that other element
where they swallow whole

masters of air and wave

o masters

a breaker collapses thins out dirties
like butter beginning to singe spreads
along the beach and flosses
to be raced at its end by my daughters shrieking

hardly a hundred yards from where the tide
storms in jumping thundering with
power which could bash a freighter
sideways onto the rocks reef it
and shift and smash it hugely again
into rusty dreaming iron
with a railed poop where somebody felt safe

UNDER MOUNT BRANDON

into the being
of those who live beneath
Brandon casts itself

with the waves of morning
the distances between common things
the local light

becoming part of the
unnoticeable landscape

MINARD CASTLE

and everyone in the car was weary
so why should I drive that far
to poke around its rectangular hulk and peer
into the fifteenth century?

and why did it does it still insist
on rising with hopeful boulders
four storeys in my mind
until I no lover of things military
must go in under the murder hole
to walk around it with words?

a whisper from ancestors
like those whose Drogheda skulls
were unearthed recently clubbed-in?

resisting holding here among their elemental
sky and the searoll the high distances the
cawing of mortality

catching its energies I became aware
of hardy Kerry eyes observing
behind a slitted ope its ingoing
a crack in time

➤

Hussey and his lost garrison

I want to look at those sad faces
listen to their Irish try
to hear what they take for granted

to measure things against the heavy keep
as Cromwell's cannons trundle nearer

and pewter bullets whirr and sink

---

pewter: when the native garrison ran out of lead, they used pewter for bullets

CUAS

the surge into this fissure
is brimming with weed from deep waters

a currach bucks at its rope
and there are cables of foam in contrails
across the mouth of the creek

where St. Brendan launched
his leather boat to discover some
new world for Christ

the same massive swell
brings fear in its spread and
rush around the pier

the kind of inlet you
might remember dying
as you could the crimson hedgerows
dripping with fuchsia up the road
the montbretia incandescent in orange

and go consoled

NOIRIN

she's well able for the men
and nods to an order
while pulling another pint

her eyes whip about with
the same mix of motives
that raises her arm and she

hardly notices the tumbling stout
though with a woman's exciting clearness
she knows her own know
would never confuse
shrewdness with intelligence

and is more than willing to hunt change
lead a visitor upstairs to
the phone that isn't out of order

talking in Irish to herself

BOITHRIN

a pause between showers and it
sends its stone echo uphill

the weathered red of galvanise belongs
and the shed with an upper door for hay

moss velvet on ancient walls

steam meanders from the culvert flags
the fresh green pats of the cows

teck a stonechat hesitates *teck teck*
holding this saturated moment

and the farmhouse eavesdrops on
a stranger's step

Bóithrín/boreen: Irish for, lane.

WARDSMAID IN DINGLE HOSPITAL

at twenty totally herself
face strong as her physique which
rebels against the regulation apron

Hoh-? she challenges
the question tossed in Irish by
an aged version of herself
(*I was like an apple in frost*)

and her response comes in a swell
and the old Gaelic kingdom is there
in a *blas* never lost to schooling

and the word is made flesh

---

blas: fluency at speaking Irish

THE VIEW IN A THOUSAND YEARS

rises near the bridge and
barely dimpling the sunny river
its reeds more or less motionless

a *caislín* hopping
at a hedge which drips with *God's tears*

the smell of unseen honeysuckle

mountains of silence
silent people
compressed by the light

and wave after wave flowering
along Ballydavid strand
with shivers of sound

as if for the first time

---

caislín : species of thrush
God's tears/ deóra Dé: Irish for, fuchsia

NEAR ANASCAUL

there comes a stillness
where the route moves upward
and the skyline begins to brighten

an intimation

APPENDIX

DUN AN OIR : Section IV (pages 28, 29)

PAGE 28

Left column : (1) look at the rope on the gallows/ Holy God/ they're going to hang us Irish/ God God, holy Mary/ and the women and children too (2) Daddy oh Daddy/ please let him alone/ he did nothing/ I beg I beseech you/ don't put that thing on him no no no no no/ that's my daddy/ my daddy (3) where is San Giuseppe (the leader)?/ what is he doing?/ I have studied in Florence/ my father my mother!/ why why why? (4) damned Fitzgerald/ where is the villain now/ and that evil Italian/ he took the sword out of our hands/ and gave us *Raleigh's mercy* instead/ I'm finished without even a fight (5) (*Epigraph from beginning of Sequence.*)

Right column: (3) (*The Sign of the Cross and start of Apostles' Creed*) (4) my ancestors lived here/ long years/ but now my tillage is burnt down/ my meadow blackened by you/ my family scattered/ I don't care whether I live or die/ the life you left us/ is only a kind of death/ I'll leave this dark existence/ gladly (5) quickly, little Mary/ go down that path/ by the side of the cliff/ before they come back/ looking for more drink/ goodbye and God bless you darling/ quick! I hear them again/ carrying the bodies

PAGE 29

Left column : (line 1) Mother of God! look at the Irish/ sir, sir, please/ I have money for you (2) listen listen/ the great darkness is crying (3) my husband my husband/ give me my grand husband/ good soldiers/ don't do that/ Mary Mother of God (4) help help help! I'm unarmed/ what about the truce?/ help me/ I'm like yourself/ take your hands off me/ cowards/ non-men/ dogs/ give me my pike villain/ and I'll fight you/ snakes / to hell with the lot of you/ Jesus Christ/ help me now

Right column (line 2) listen to them kicking/ the poor people/ I'm going mad/ I'll jump off the cliff/ I'd prefer that/ to this awful crucifixion (3) mercy mercy/ take your hand off me/ take your hand off me/ oh God God (4) stay with me Tom my son/ they won't touch you/ believe me/ I won't let them/ stay with me child/ stay with me (5) long live the Pope (6) God save Ireland